OVIRAPTOR

by Janet Riehecky
illustrated by Diana Magnuson

THE CHILD'S WORLD

MANKATO, MN

*Grateful appreciation is expressed to
Bret S. Beall, Research Consultant,
Field Museum of Natural History, Chicago,
Illinois, who reviewed this book to
insure its accuracy.*

Library of Congress Cataloging in Publication Data

Riehecky, Janet, 1953-
    Oviraptor / by Janet Riehecky ; illustrated by Diana Magnuson.
        p. cm. — (Dinosaur books)
    Summary: Describes known and hypothesized information about the
dinosaur Oviraptor, including physical appearance and lifestyle.
    ISBN 0-89565-631-0.
    1. Oviraptor—Juvenile literature.   [1. Oviraptor.
2. Dinosaurs.]   I. Magnuson, Diana, ill.   II. Title.   III. Series:
Riehecky, Janet, 1953-   Dinosaur books.
QE862.S3R537   1990
567.9'7—dc20   90-42926
                                                                    CIP
                                                                    AC

OVIRAPTOR

Dinosaurs ruled the land when they
lived millions of years ago, but they
weren't the only animals that lived back
then.

The skies were full of all kinds of creatures.

There were many kinds of strange rep-
tiles that glided through the sky, some
with long tails . . .

and some with large crests on their heads.

The very first bird lived back then.

And as time passed, many other birds
shared the earth with the dinosaurs.

None of these creatures were dinosaurs, but scientists think all of them were related to the dinosaurs. One type of dinosaur that makes them think this is the Oviraptor (O-vih-RAP-tor).

The Oviraptor was a small dinosaur with a very strange head. It measured only five or six feet from the tip of its tail to the top of its head and stood just three or four feet tall. It was also very slender, weighing only about sixty pounds. That was just a single mouthful for the terrible Tyrannosaurus!

The Oviraptor was a dinosaur, but in many ways it was like a bird. Some scientists even think it had feathers!

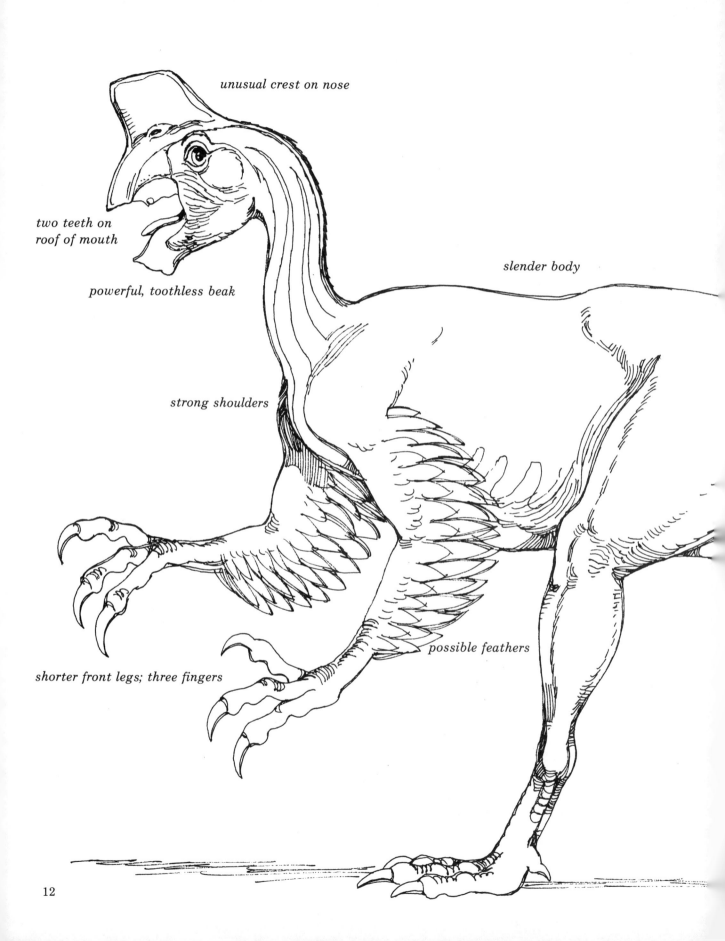

unusual crest on nose

two teeth on
roof of mouth

powerful, toothless beak

slender body

strong shoulders

shorter front legs; three fingers

possible feathers

12

The legs, feet, and body of the Oviraptor were similar in many ways to a bird's. The legs were long and slender with three large toes and a small side toe on each foot. The toes had long claws and might have been roughly scaled, like a chicken's.

The Oviraptor did not have wings, but its front legs (or arms) may have had feathers on them. The body was slender and shaped like that of a bird. But the Oviraptor didn't look exactly like today's birds. It had a long, thick tail like a lizard's. Can you imagine a robin with a lizard's tail?

long, slender back legs

three long toes with claws; one side toe

The head of the Oviraptor was different from any other dinosaur's. It was shaped something like a flamingo's head with a parrot's beak. It had one eye on each side of its head, as many birds do. Seeing something different with each eye helped the Oviraptor watch out for danger.

On the roof of its mouth, the Oviraptor had two strange teeth—not a row of teeth in its jaws, but just two teeth in the middle of the roof of its mouth. Scientists are puzzled about what the Oviraptor could have used those two teeth for.

On its nose, the Oviraptor had a large, unusual crest. Scientists aren't sure what the crest was used for either. Perhaps a male Oviraptor showed off with it to get the attention of a female, as many birds do. That crest was certainly strange enough to make any animal look twice.

The jaws and beak of the Oviraptor were very strong, but unusual in shape. The Oviraptor didn't have the sharp teeth of a meat eater, but its mouth wasn't like that of most plant eaters either. Scientists think the Oviraptor probably ate anything it could get—fruit, leaves, insects, lizards, and small mammals. It may even have waited until a big meat eater finished its meal and then slipped in to see if there was anything left it could grab.

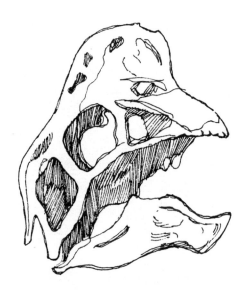

Many scientists think the Oviraptor was good at stealing one food in particular —the eggs of other dinosaurs. In fact, the name Oviraptor means "egg stealer" or "egg thief." Eggs are a favorite food of many animals, and the beak of the Ovirap-

tor could crunch through an egg shell easily. The three-fingered hands and strong arms of the Oviraptor were probably good at digging in the sand to find and grab eggs.

But, of course, it was dangerous to sneak into a dinosaur's nest and steal the eggs—the mother dinosaur usually objected! In fact, the very first skeleton ever found of an Oviraptor was found with a nest of Protoceratops eggs. We don't know for sure, but it seems likely that the egg thief got caught in the act!

Even if the Oviraptor was just minding its own business, other dinosaurs probably tried to catch it anyway—to eat it. Meat eaters such as Velociraptor and Troodon might have dined frequently on Oviraptors.

Oviraptor's best defense probably was to run. Its long, strong legs seemed made just for that! Few dinosaurs could catch the Oviraptor on open ground.

But sometimes an Oviraptor got itself trapped. If it did, it put up a big fight. The claws on its feet and hands were very sharp, and it could bite hard with its beak. However, when faced with a fierce meat eater, the Oviraptor would often lose.

Oviraptors lived near the end of the age of dinosaurs. Some scientists used to believe that this little egg thief helped bring about the end of the dinosaurs. They thought Oviraptors and other creatures ate so many eggs that dinosaurs died out. Few, if any, scientists think this anymore. But they can't agree on what did kill the dinosaurs.

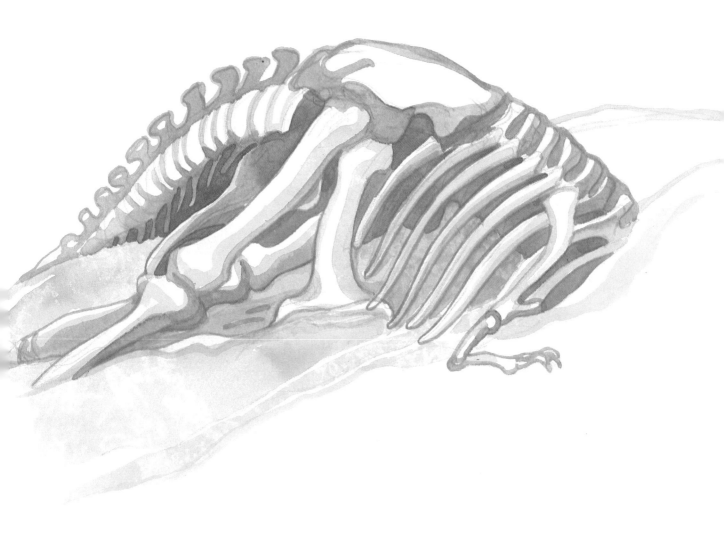

Some scientists think the dinosaurs died out little by little because of a disease or a change in the food supply. Other scientists argue that creatures that lived successfully on earth for one hundred and forty million years could not have been killed so easily.

Some scientists think that the temperature of the earth gradually changed, becoming either much hotter or much colder, and that this killed the dinosaurs. This idea makes some sense, but again, it seems too small a cause to have killed every single dinosaur.

Many scientists think a huge asteroid or meteorite from space crashed into the earth, causing the end of the age of dinosaurs. Such a disaster might have raised a dust cloud that covered the entire earth, blocking out the sunlight for months or even years. The darkness would

have killed many plants and changed the temperature of the earth. These things might have worked together to kill the dinosaurs. Many scientists believe this is what happened, but no one can say for sure.

We will probably never know exactly what happened. But it's still fun to imagine what the world was like when the dinosaurs lived!

Dinosaur Fun

Would you like to learn more about dinosaurs? A good place to start is at your library or local bookstore. Look for these books to help you discover more about dinosaurs:

The Big Beast Book: Dinosaurs and How They Got That Way, by Jerry Booth

The Big Book of Dinosaurs: A Natural History of the Prehistoric World, by Dougal Dixon

Dinosaur (Eyewitness Books), by David Norman and Angela Milner

A Field Guide to Dinosaurs: The First Complete Guide to Every Dinosaur Now Known, by David Lambert

When Dinosaurs Ruled the Earth, by David Norman